T0118102

indwelling

**Gillian Allnutt** was born in 1949 in London but spent half of her childhood in Newcastle upon Tyne. In 1988 she returned to live in the North East. Before that, she read Philosophy and English at Cambridge and then spent the next 17 years living mostly in London, working mostly as a part-time teacher in further and adult education but also as a performer, publisher, journalist and freelance editor. From 1983 to 1988 she was Poetry Editor at *City Limits* magazine.

Her collections *Nantucket and the Angel* and *Lintel* were both shortlisted for the T.S. Eliot Prize. Poems from these collections are included in her Bloodaxe retrospective *How the Bicycle Shone: New & Selected Poems* (2007), which draws on six published books plus a new collection, *Wolf Light*, and was a Poetry Book Society Special Commendation. Her most recent collections, both from Bloodaxe, are *indwelling* (2013) and *wake* (2018). She has also published *Berthing: A Poetry Workbook* (NEC/Virago, 1991), and was co-editor of *The New British Poetry* (Paladin, 1988).

From 2001 to 2003 she held a Royal Literary Fund Fellowship at Newcastle and Leeds Universities. She won the Northern Rock Foundation Writer's Award in 2005 and received a Cholmondeley Award in 2010. Since 1983 she has taught creative writing in a variety of contexts, mainly in adult education and as a writer in schools. In 2009/10 she held a writing residency with The Medical Foundation for the Care of Victims of Torture (now Freedom From Torture) in the North East, working with asylum seekers in Newcastle and Stockton. In 2013/14 she taught creative writing to undergraduates on the Poetry and Poetics course in the English Department of Durham University. She lives in Co. Durham.

Gillian Allnutt was awarded the Queen's Gold Medal for Poetry 2016. The Medal is given for excellence in poetry and was presented to her by The Queen.

# GILLIAN ALLNUTT

# indwelling

BLOODAXE BOOKS

Copyright © Gillian Allnutt 2013

ISBN: 978 1 85224 980 9

First published 2013 by
Bloodaxe Books Ltd,
Highgreen,
Tarset,
Northumberland NE48 1RP.

www.bloodaxebooks.com
For further information about Bloodaxe titles
please visit our website or write to
the above address for a catalogue.

Supported by
**ARTS COUNCIL
ENGLAND**

LEGAL NOTICE

All rights reserved. No part of this book may be
reproduced, stored in a retrieval system, or
transmitted in any form, or by any means, electronic,
mechanical, photocopying, recording or otherwise,
without prior written permission from Bloodaxe Books Ltd.

Requests to publish work from this book
must be sent to Bloodaxe Books Ltd.

Gillian Allnutt has asserted her right under
Section 77 of the Copyright, Designs and Patents Act 1988
to be identified as the author of this work.

Cover design: Neil Astley & Pamela Robertson-Pearce.

Digital reprint of the 2013 Bloodaxe Books edition.

*for Nansi Morgan*

The wind bloweth where it listeth, and thou hearest the
sound thereof, but canst not tell whence it cometh, and
whither it goeth: so is every one that is born of the Spirit.

JOHN 3,8

GREENHAM SONG

You can't kill the Spirit.
She is like a mountain.
Old and strong,
She goes on and on and on.

# ACKNOWLEDGEMENTS

Acknowledgements are due to the editors of the following publications in which some of these poems first appeared: *A Speaking Silence: Quaker Poets of Today* (Indigo Dreams Publishing, 2013), *The Best British Poetry 2011* (Salt Publishing, 2011), *Contourlines: New Responses to Landscape in Word and Image* (Salt Publishing in association with Magdalene College Publications, 2009), *Granta, How Things Are Made: Poems for Gordon Hodgeon* (Square One Books, 2009), *The North, Poetry Ireland Review, Poetry London, Poetry Review, Poetry Wales, The Rialto, The Ropes* (Diamond Twig, 2008), *Southlight, The Spectator, Uncurtained Windows* (Soaring Penguin, 2013).

'Earth' appeared on the Ledbury Poetry Festival website (www.poetry-festival.co.uk) in 2008.

I'd like to thank The Society of Authors for a Cholmondeley Award in 2010.

And I'd like to thank both New Writing North and The Medical Foundation for the Care of Victims of Torture (now Freedom From Torture) in the North East for making possible the residency I did with the latter in 2009/10.

# CONTENTS

STEPPE

# BOXTED

# Elsbeth

*After the painting,* Elsbeth, *1902, by Paula Modersohn-Becker*

In Russia a saint came out of an egg.

Like a bird, Father said.

Like a rag.

Boris or Gleb or Basil.

Will you paint my soul?

It's laid.

Mother is ill, with her candle.

The cost of light is not inconsiderable.

Father's word.

Have you a word for me like a wheelbarrow handle?

In 1901 Paula Becker married fellow-painter Otto Modersohn, whose first wife had died. Elsbeth was the daughter of his earlier marriage.

# The Quiet Parisian

*After* A Corner of the Artist's Room in Paris *by Gwen John*


the *bloc à dessin*

the anterior rude stone, Rodin

the curtain, light, full-length

without, the *quartier*

anxiety, the family

the heart's milk wood made welcome

as necessity

as strength of will

as summer in a jamjar on the table

.


*bloc à dessin:* drawing-block.

# Morning Room

*After* Interior with Girl Reading, *1908, by Peter Ilsted*


We'd battle for the mirror, later on.

For morning, broken.

Mab, alone, without reflection

Wanted not to be among.

A web, what if, walked through.

A letter from.

Then war came with its great gun like an old Gran trundling.

## drawing

a little saucepan set

*ad hoc*, like the heart, the wedding-day of doubt

a study for it

# Conversation with a Woman from the Orthodox Jewish Community

*Gateshead, 2004*


*He led me under the canopy* she said.

I knew her as one who'd come back unaccompanied after the war

but when she said *the way he asked: 'Would you like to live with
    my father?'*

the war gave way in my heart forever

as if we'd been on the road to Emmaus

as if we'd been on the bus

together.

In the Jewish wedding ceremony the bride and groom stand under a canopy.

## The Sisters

*After the painting by Stanley Spencer*

### *The Younger*

I remember the worst, the mast, those small winged cases.

How they stayed on the tree for ever.

How they stayed themselves in air.

How they'd lost their heart's desire.

How they stayed all winter.

Odd, how voluble they were.

How still, the world's edge there.

Where we'd found fumitory before.

I was always with her.

Hauled, as if I were broken, on three wheels.

As if I were a three-legged stool.

I offered to fetch one for her.

I would have climbed the tree for her.

She didn't hear.

Those little empty cases didn't interest her.

Those little ears.

## The Older

At first she wasn't there.

I can imagine land and sea and sky, the undivided.

Moon, all mine.

Moon alone and a sad man looking out of her.

Moon with its lanthorn.

Pyramus and Thisbe could have done, whatever they did, without her.

Shakespeare.

Where did we go, that first midsummer?

To Grandmother.

*Motherless girls now, Mary, Martha.*

She said it to anyone who'd have tea with her.

Agnes and Elsie in their tat.

The little black perched hats.

Veiled, as if they never would forget the war.

*We managed well enough before.*

Well enough without her.

I *like* my winged hair.

# Her Stroke

*(in memory of my grandmother)*


She lay alone and her hair in long loose braids undone

where she had been.

She would insist

it was August.

The war had taken

John

and left her Imperial Leather,

the beautiful old oval mirror that had been her mother's.

*Daddy's in the doings again*

she said, hearing the chain.


John, my mother's older brother, was killed in 1943.

# my mother, her brother

as to the husk of her –

husk, little house –

who was houselled, here, among fields
at Thornham Parva –

death was older
death stood up for her
death disfigured her

whose saints were of an earlier –

delicate, brisk

as straw

The Thornham Parva Retable dates from around 1330 and was originally made for Thetford Priory. It disappeared at the Dissolution. When it resurfaced in a local stable loft in the 1920s, it was donated to Thornham Parva Church. Eight saints are depicted on this panelled altar-piece. And see note to previous poem.

# Mother

her nest of thin air –

Gabriel, who came seeking her
who was here, there –

but for the great white gift of her
agoraphobia –

his wings, his grandeur –

girlhood, left her –
little church, of thatch, of Thornham Parva

whilom, whilom –

what was lost to her –

history –

some of the Paston Letters, say

A collection of letters preserved by the Pastons, a well-to-do Norfolk family,
were written between *c*. 1420 and 1503.

## the child

the parable

the pebble, pondered, if at all –

the layette and the *dear Lord God* of it

the beauty of the opened basket

the accustomed chair, the kept, quiet hour

the root, the uproot, of her –

Perry Rise and Perry Vale

the rote of the heart

the heart's roundel

*all shall be well*

*and all manner of thing shall be well* –

the child's

the rudest and most rudimentary of the worlds

Lines 10 & 11 are quoted from Julian of Norwich: *Revelations of Divine Love*, translated by Christian Wolters (Penguin, 1966).

# Boxted

*Agatha*

I, the middle one, am

Pestle, mortar.

I polish them,

Mother,

As if they were my own

Who bide where I from time to time –

Your poor apostles, brother

Spoons.

Iscariot alone –

You'd marry

The man who made them for your wedding-day.

Here's Simon

Peter, James, the son of Zebedee, and John –

Broad-shouldered men.

## Abiko

Agatha, making an epithalamium

In the middle garden.

Agatha, polishing spoons

Like Mother. I

Am curlew-thin.

Am dry

As moon, as moor, in May.

Am early-morning thin.

Shadows of box and cedar, thickened,

Sit through sermons.

Words, made over.

Mother

Sickened when. *When I*

*Am laid.*

## *Abut*

Am but.

Am old as doubt.

Am oak, box, thorn

Uncut.

Am not

Among apostles, am alone.

The Kingdom of God – a box of wood, worm.

Am a ward of court.

About. About

A thicket of doubt

Abiko walks, among worn books, wearing her skirt of long john silver

Without.

Am an attached hamlet.

Am, but.

*Boxted*: a village in Suffolk.

*Abiko*: *abiku* are spirit children, born to live for only a short while before returning to the idyllic world of their spirit companions. See *The Famished Road* by Ben Okri.

*When I am laid*: from Dido's Lament in Purcell's opera *Dido and Aeneas*.

## Daft Sister

Went to the hovel.

Wanted to show her the hollyhock.

Its yellow flower towered above her.

Dared, she dared back.


Still, the water-butt. Shadows, where.

Nor here, nor there.

For hours.


Mother, because of her.

Left.


In her tower of laughter, lightly.


Lied about going down the lane.

Lied about a lizard on a stone.

Lied about the water level.

Lied about the sun.


A tower of Babel lying on its side.

A table, laid.

## Sorrow

It's young.

It goes back to the earth's beginning.

To the earth belonging.

To her.

Its feet, everywhere, on the parquet floor.

Maud, the world over.

The sea attaches itself to her.

An old medallion, the moon, reflects upon her.

Aristocratic.

A lost demesne.

On its delicate light chain, her lizard, her loon.

## the shawl

*(in memoriam Julia Darling)*

of air and wool

her frail earthwhile

who promised her people

palanquin, purple and pall

and left them all

a little something fit for April

snowfall

# Delft Lass

*After* A Woman and Her Maid in a Courtyard, *c. 1660 by Pieter de Hooch*

Nothing deft about her.

Nothing daft either.

Nevertheless.

Not cut out for.

Misses her mother.

There is unevenness in her, as of cloud.

Thin, Netherlandish.

As if she'd never handled.

A light dish.

# haar

*(for Janet Moody)*

nuns moor, near

where the allotments are

like boats at

unabated

now is the hospital hour

the loss of her hair

an old grey horse, the haar

near, near

the lustre of air

wild rose of earliest summer

loss, entrusted to her

*at the hour shaped for him Scyld*

there is no other shore

*Haar*, a cold sea-fog; *Nuns Moor*, open ground in the centre of Newcastle; *Scyld*, from *Beowulf*, translated by Michael Alexander (Penguin, 1973).

# in her kitchen

*(for Janet Moody)*

delphinium

the heart, fleet, in its large domain

a *grand meaulnes*

summer, recalled, a light blue lent sea

of dust and shadow, now, the house

of doubtfulness

who, in the hospital, implored them –

deep in daylight, implicate, a crowd

hours pass, unrecalled

the heart, a striped tent in a field

*Le Grand Meaulnes:* a novel by Alain-Fournier.

# Stranger

World, athwart –

the sack of it.

*How many hundredweight – ?*

Child, in a good coat, awkward and thick.

Asylum, St Nicholas'. Black stone. Light –

a stack of it.

Two pairs of knickers on, pulled up.

Shop. The one shop, Isaac Walton.

*Yes we can, no we can't, alter it.*

La Sagesse, the nun at the gate.

In her shadow, the harlot. Laughter –

the lack of it.

*Newcastle, November 1956*

*St Nicholas'*, the mental hospital.
*La Sagesse*, the convent school.
*Isaac Walton's*, the shop that stocked the uniform.

# STOUP

## Earth

The ache of having.

Hard of –

Sanity, a helmet, stops you hearing things.

The lucid talk of stones.

The sea, aloud.

The whole word–

Hoard.

Having bone.

You might break your shoulder again.

# Shore

Am, the oncoming.

*My courteous Lord* –

Scattered, the proud.

*Finisterre*'s but a field of –

Fear, a whore –

among the already occluded worlds

she'll make her home.

*My courteous Lord:* an affectionate form of address to God by Julian of Norwich. See note on page 21.

# her dwelling

*After* La Femme au Chapelet *by* Cézanne


soul-poor, the sill

as conscience clear, the well

between sabot and star the hovel where

ever, in kindle

the river

the stone-pine with its roughened shadow, dour

Sainte-Victoire with its one good shoulder


*Saint-Victoire:* the mountain painted many times by Cézanne.

# Asylum

Where chimneys, long-black, for her, lunatic, have waited.

Fog adheres.

For her, *Magnificat* and cardboard, staidly

Lit.

For her, soot, laidly.

Soot, like stars.

Where evensong is said.

# Coronation

By and by, the balustrade.

We waited quietly for the Queen who wasn't there, whose car –

The moon of alabaster.

*Light of men*

that lay across her throat, a thwart scar.

Bitter, the heart's sweet thought of –

Nothing but

the gold abyss of God.

We waited, quietly, for.

The flying buttress of the sea, put by.

*Because they have taken away my Lord, and I –*

l.2: Summer, 1953: we waited in front of my great-aunt's house in New Cross, South London, to wave to the Queen as she was driven past in an open-topped car.
l.4: John 1. 4.
l.11: John 20. 13.

# Scarecrow, winter

*Then said Jesus, Let her alone*
JOHN 12. 7


Absence inhabit her, here, among men.

Absence, a moved stone.

Let her be cast, clout.

Magnificat.

By a garden of apple and elder bared.

Of all but the loveliest, burd.

Calendula quicken her.

Snow, caul, cover the prescience in her.

# Lyke-Wake

Lichen.

The astounded simplicity of stone.

The word alone

inlaid.

Middlesbrough.

A leaf that, one year withered, was as if it were

made lace of air.

It is a ghost's ear, said the girl.

Love, loaned her.

Mother Teresa, when you pray, what do you say to God?

I don't say anything, she said.

I listen.

God?

God listens too, she said.

Astonied

Lord, inlaid.

# My Seventeenth-century Girlhood

My soul, lint.

*I saw three ships come sailing by on Christmas Day, on Christmas Day*

anent –

The Lord's Prayer, thick like worsted, pocketed.

Our Father, said.

Simnel, my mother said –

*a pottle of Milk, half a pint of good Sack.*

My lyke, lent.

A pottle is 4 pints or half a gallon, about 2 litres.
*a pottle of Milk, half a pint of good Sack* is from a recipe for spice cake in
*A True Gentlewoman's Delight* by The Countess of Kent, first published in
1653 and quoted in *English Bread and Yeast Cookery* by Elizabeth David.

## but for

the baffle of my father

would have called her

would have called her star by star as if an orchestra

all that cafuffle

would have crossed Baikal

*for those in peril*

for her

*for those in peril:* from the hymn 'Eternal Father Strong to Save' by William Whiting of Winchester, 1860.

## shaman

mother mary ambrose blue

before the maze, the amaze, of stars, I –

earth, all hers –

the hour of lapis lazuli

the whore, necessity

the snow, *les neiges d'antan*, I knew

I'd known her, always, by

*les neiges d'antan* is from the 'Ballade des dames du temps jadis' by François
Villon (*b*. 1431).

**now**

the quiet carousel of the snow

# Elisabeth

In the night, great with stars, there is room for her, death, adoration –

I, that am ignorant, stone, shall be extinguished, one by one –

that am Zachary –

Luke 1. 5-24 and 57-79.

## stoup

like home

the worn towel on a woman's arm

Armenia, Lake Sevan

the heart, whole, hollowed

out of harm

## duduk

my heart
      led out
            among the iliads of light

*duduk*: a traditional woodwind instrument, originally from Armenia.

# Joy

Let it assemble.

Let it resemble itself alone.

On the road to Emmaus

*Did not our heart burn within us?*

From the unassimilable, stone, of apricot

*Eau de Noyaux.*

Let none dissemble it.

*Did not our heart burn within us?* Luke, 24. 32

## earth

a small pavilion

a summer's afternoon

for John

a slow air, borne

or liminal, a skin

a little something

to put on

## Lullaby

Consider the lilies of the field

how they are not beguiled

how they are whiled away

how the world, awry

how *the faucon hath borne my mak away*

how the beck flows by and by

The quoted line is from *Corpus Christi*, a fifteenth-century carol.

# STEPPE

# In the Botanic Garden, Oxford

*Gateway in the Wall*

Five thousand pounds to *the glorification of God* given

that a physic garden might grow within

biding, as stone bides, in sun and rain,

a boon.


But for the paper cone to which wasps hasten,

but for *Henricus Comes Danby*, whose inscription,

but for *caritas*, heart's courtesy,

common.

## Black Pine

involved, in this early garden, almost

beyond expectation, or aspersion, cast

poor Tolkien with his talk of Bilbo Baggins

pocketful of fustian, man

who, nevertheless

*Surely the darkness shall cover me*

darkness at noon

in the delta of my heart

in the remote, platitudinous rivers of my bark

in my upright, almost

in my involution

not that I was ever or lately in Threadneedle Street, London

*English Yew, planted 1645*


halt, your shadow-haul


your soul hid in your shoulder


sherpaless


### Gateway in the Wall
Sir Henry Danvers gave £5,000 to set up a physic garden for 'the glorification of God and for the furtherance of learning'. The walls and arches were built on such a grand scale that by the time they were finished in 1633 all the money had been spent.

### Black Pine
*Pinus nigra* var. *nigra*. The seed was collected in Northern Europe in 1790; the resulting sapling was planted out in 1800.
It was the favourite tree of J.R.R. Tolkien.
*Surely the darkness shall cover me*: Psalm 139. 11.

### English Yew, planted 1645
The oldest tree in the Garden, planted by Jacob Bobart. Because for many years it was clipped into a variety of shapes, it is not as large as a yew tree of that age should be.

# It is always the last summer

Unwalled, garden of thrift and fret.

There are fewer winkles where, upon the rock.

He turns back.


Dust on the pane and then.

The Caledonian Road. The sudden old smell of rain on paving-stone.

Startles one.


One whittles the world from her father's feet.

The stone, as yet.

Which says *Dold*. Which may not be right.


The wireless accompanies them.

It plays music by Khatchaturian.

Whereupon.


A woman is washed up out of the whitening.


They go to look at the bones.

Siberian bones.

In Whitechapel, where they are shown.

# To let my father go

*Lord, now*

Straiten this now in me worldward: according to rule

His shoulder, slurred, I rode then

*Up and down the City Road, in and out the Eagle*

His untoward shoulder

*Go, said the bird*

'You sang' he told me 'like a small bird, Israel, by the water'

*Lord, now*

Loud

The let-my-people-go-ward of his shoulder


*Lord, now lettest thou thy servant depart in peace: according to thy word* is the opening of the *Nunc Dimittis* which is part of Evening Prayer in *The Book of Common Prayer.*

*Up and down the City Road, in and out the Eagle* is from the nursery rhyme *Pop Goes the Weasel.*

*Go, said the bird* is from T.S. Eliot's 'Burnt Norton', the first of his *Four Quartets.*

# Shostakovich

*After* Twenty-four Preludes and Fugues *for piano*

His days, considered, one by one.

His days of cloud and bone.

His each day.

His

For what the snow would all too soon lay bare of birch, of being.

Johann Sebastian.

Bare wooden box of music paper

Kept by him.

Pestilential, summer.

That old portrait of his –

Who'd lay bare the loneliness of loving.

Shostakovich's *Preludes and Fugues* were inspired by his study of Bach, in particular *The Well-Tempered Clavier*. They were written in 1950-51.

# His Library

Linden by linden laid down.

Residuum.

*Am an attendant lord*, Lord Chamberlain.

No one has opened them.

A small wind flies about the room.

It is out of Africa.

The map of the heart, anterior.

The heron. The hour.

*When Herod the king.*

His deposition.

Days, unscholarly, unschooled.

*Non serviam.*

The wood spool of the world.


*Am an attendant Lord:* from Eliot's 'The Love Song of J. Alfred Prufrock'.
*When Herod the king:* Matthew 2. 3.
*Non serviam:* the traditional declaration of Satan..

# Sibelius

The forests discern him,

the forests of idle turbulent rain,

whose horses, bridled, barely,

whose chariots, burn.

Jean Sibelius's tone poem *Night-ride and Sunrise* was written in 1909 and the symphonic poem *Tapiola* in 1925.

# Contumely

his wherewithal

his shadow, walled, as that of Ivan the Terrible

walled, without ear

hen in the *shtetl* hidden, he called her

his small Siberia

## Immersion

colour of Baikal

through which the stone fell

ever, ever

shame, the reservoir

someone is calling her

colour of the at home in her

someone or other

Shem, Ham

# In Armenia

As if he were the unforgiven, flowered.

As if he were the hour.

As if with his mother.

As if he were the scoured earth floor.

As if he were plucking the few poor apricots from the path of the wind.

As if he were putting them in her hand.

As if she'd been watching him from the door.

## Ilse

Then I lived by water –

winter


in my breathing, bone

white, thin –


alone

and without other occupation.


Hamburg burned. I heard

they boarded


trains. In cardboard cases. Children.

None.


Imagine

when the wind blew clean


a benison.

No other kin.

# infather

the moot, immutable places of the mind –

the heritable mind –

*remembered, if outlived*

as belsen

burned

The quoted line is from Emily Dickinson's poem 'After great pain, a formal feeling comes – '.
In May 1945 my father's army regiment took part in burning down Belsen.

## 'love to burn him down like belsen'

*(i.m. my father)*


love to burn him down like belsen

in her arms, the had man

her asylum

flame

See note to the previous poem.

## his cello

and this is how I imagine it came to him –

early one morning, a tumbrel or cart

quiet as a nailed crate
quiet as a wood
quiet, an abyss, embodied –

who would not have been abhorred by it

Pablo Casals, 1876-1973

## the one

who bought the house

the *jas de bouffan*

the habitation of the wind

by whom I was

who owned

the mountain

hat in hand

Louis-Auguste Cézanne (1798-1886), father of the painter, worked in the hat trade before setting up a bank in Aix-en-Provence and making a good deal of money. During his lifetime he supported his son with reluctance but after his death, Cézanne was able to paint without worrying again about money.

## 'the wind like glass'

the wind like glass

a white shadow

clarity

which too will pass

# Steppe

As if it were abroad in her.

Her heart, a troika.

The floor of fine board bright as ever.

As before the war.

Sobriety, bone china, in her.

In Isaiah.

But the boy, lame, neither here nor there.

Alone in one another.

Plywood, paper, aeroplane.

Something must have cleared the air between them.

There is shame in her.

She's thinner.

You could come upon her of a sudden.

As if the moon had risen.

As if the horses had been heard by someone.

# Kiril, before him

the small blue silence of the flower

the silence of Siberia

Baikal, the reservoir

the silence, spatulate, of water

St Cyril (826-69) and St Methodius (815-85), brothers, were known as the
Apostles of the Slavs. Cyril gave his name to the Cyrillic alphabet, becoming
the founder of Slavonic literature and of Old Church Slavonic.

Printed in the USA
CPSIA information can be obtained
at www.ICGtesting.com
JSHW082225140824
68134JS00015B/744

9 781852 249809